T0042165

VIKING VOYAGES

PATHFINDER EDITION

By Fran Downey and Amy Ostenso

CONTENTS

VIKING VOYAGES

By Fran Downey

For nearly 300 years, the Vikings sparked fear in their enemies. The Vikings were fearless warriors who stormed villages, attacked fortresses, stole gold, and captured slaves.

Not all Vikings, however, were villains. Some were farmers and craftspeople, while others discovered new lands. They were the first Europeans to sail to North America, but their story is lost in the mists of the past. Now it's time to meet the real Vikings.

All stories have beginnings.

This one is no different. It begins on June 8, 793, the day Viking ships sailed southwest toward a small **island** off the coast of England.

It wasn't long before the island's **inhabitants** spotted the ships, although they were still far away. It was impossible for the island's people to see who was onboard.

No one knew what was about to happen, nor did they know that a new chapter in history was opening. They could only wait—and wonder.

Cool Cup. *Vikings used ox horns like the one above as cups on special occasions.*

Rowing Ashore

The ships, each carrying a hundred men, came closer. Some of the men operated long oars, plunging them into the water. As the men pulled on the oars, the boats lurched forward.

Alongside the oarsmen sat fierce warriors. Each fighter wore a heavy metal helmet. Some were carrying swords while others held axes. All were eager to invade the island.

That's exactly what they did. As soon as the ships touched the shore, the warriors jumped out and looted the island. They took everything of value, loading their ships with treasure. Then they sailed away and into history.

The attack on the island was the first Viking raid and the beginning of the Viking Age. For the next three centuries, people living along the coast of Europe would dread the appearance of Viking ships.

Village Life

Vikings are best known for their ships and daring sea adventures; yet most never went to sea. Many lived in small villages on land that now lies in Denmark, Norway, and Sweden.

Walls surrounded some of the villages, keeping enemies out. Inside the walls, people went about their daily lives. Many worked as merchants and craftspeople, buying and selling goods that other Vikings had plundered from faraway lands.

Villagers constructed houses. Builders stuck large posts into the ground and wove branches through the posts. Then they smeared mud over the branches and used soil to make the roof.

Unfriendly Faces. *This artwork shows Viking raiders around the year 1100.*

On the Farm

Most Vikings lived on farms, however, not in villages. They grew vegetables, such as peas and cabbage, and raised cattle. They ate beef and lamb and drank milk from cows, sheep, and goats.

Viking life was busy because there was always work to do. The growing season was short, and winters were long. Farmers had to make sure they had enough food to last through the cold, harsh winters.

Still, Vikings enjoyed sports and other entertainments. They liked to ski and swim. They also played chess and another game similar to checkers.

They practiced their religion, too. Vikings believed in many gods, including Odin, the king of their gods. He soared through the sky on an eight-legged horse. Thor was another god. Vikings always knew when he was nearby. They thought lightning flashed and thunder boomed as Thor rode his chariot across the sky.

Some of the names for the days of the week come from these gods. For example, Thursday comes from a Viking word meaning Thor's day and Friday comes from Frigg's day. Frigg was Odin's wife.

Sod Houses. *Vikings may have lived in houses like these.*

Lord of Thunder. *This statue shows Thor, who was the Viking god of thunder and lightning. He also battled against giants.*

Ship Ahoy!

Viking villages were similar to many villages at the time. Their ships, however, were entirely different. Viking ships were engineering marvels for their day. No one else had anything like them. Indeed, the Vikings owed much of their success to their shipbuilders.

Each ship was built for speed. The hulls were designed to glide over waves, which made them faster than ships that just plowed through the water. Large colorful sails caught the wind, pushing the ships over open water. Some of the sails were 40 feet across.

When ships advanced close to shore or up rivers, the Vikings lowered the sails and used the oars. Ships had up to 50 oars.

These speedy vessels were large, some more than 90 feet in length. They could transport both warriors and horses.

Viking Coins.
Vikings loved their ships. In fact, they put pictures of them on their money!

VIKING SHIP

Vikings used the sail to glide over the open sea. Close to shore or on rivers, they used the oars to row the ship.

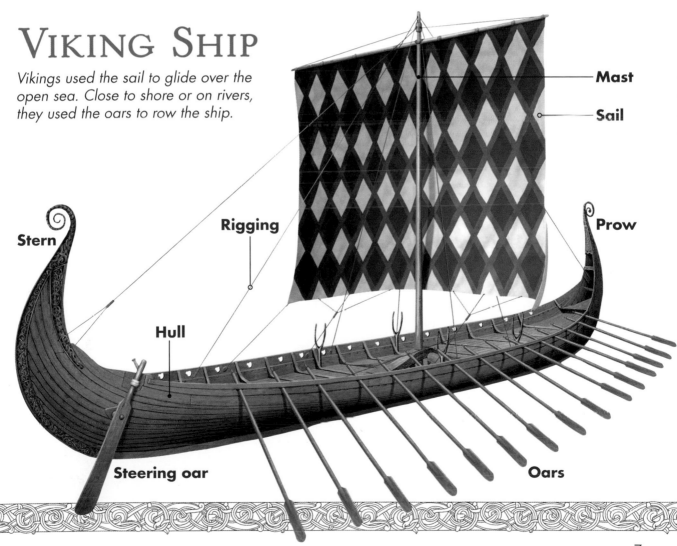

Mast

Sail

Rigging

Stern

Prow

Hull

Steering oar

Oars

The Discoverers

Some Viking men left their wives, families, and homes to go on long **voyages** that frequently lasted for years. These amazing journeys took them to faraway lands.

Vikings sailed to England, France, Spain, and Italy, as well as to Africa and Asia. They were also the first Europeans to come to the **continent** of North America.

The trip to North America was slow and had several stops along the way. In 860, Vikings reached the island of Iceland. Many years later, in 982, a Viking named Erik the Red discovered Greenland.

New Lands

These were exciting times. Vikings were discovering new lands and moving to new places. Then came word of a sighting of uncharted land. Erik the Red wanted to go to this place, but he never carried out his plan. On the way to his ship, Erik fell off his horse. Fearing bad luck, he canceled the trip.

Erik's son, Leif Eriksson, did make the trip. About 1000, he not only spotted the new land; he went ashore. He named the place Vinland. It was the East Coast of North America. He probably sailed along the coast and may even have sailed to what is now New York City.

Vinland Voyagers. *The painting below shows Viking settlers landing at Vinland shortly after the year 1000.*

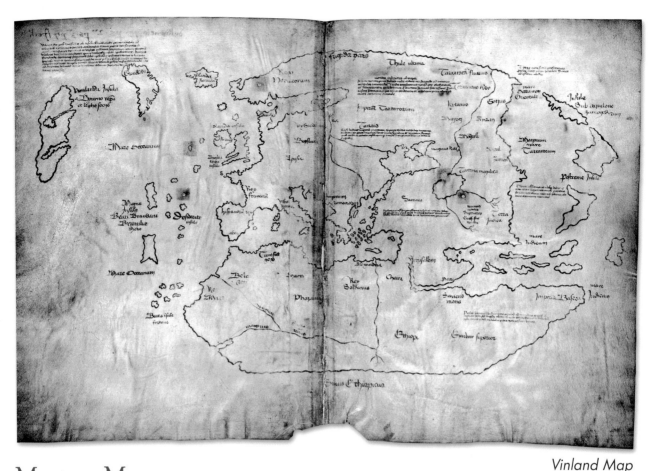

Vinland Map

Mystery Map

There is much evidence that Vikings settled in North America. Ancient legends tell of their Vinland adventures. Archaeologists have found a Viking village in Canada, and there may even be a Viking map that shows Vinland.

The map is a bit faded, but you can see parts of Europe clearly drawn. You can also see Iceland and Greenland. Beyond those islands is Vinland. It doesn't look much like North America today. After all, Vikings were only familiar with a small portion of the continent.

Not everyone agrees that Vikings drew this map. Some think it's a fake and point out that it is the only known map showing Viking discoveries in North America. Why would they make just one map? No one knows.

The map is just one more mystery about the Vikings' never-ending story. Scientists are still searching for more clues about the Vikings' past. Perhaps we will never know their full story. Yet one thing is certain. The Vikings' colorful stories are an important part of American history.

WORDWISE

continent: large landmass

inhabitant: person who lives in a place

island: a piece of land that is completely surrounded by water

voyage: a long trip on a ship

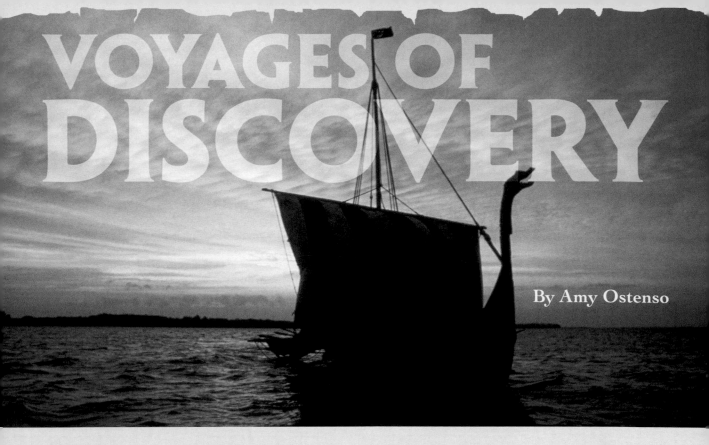

VOYAGES OF DISCOVERY

By Amy Ostenso

When Viking warriors sailed down the coast of Europe raiding settlements, they took gold and other valuables. But Erik the Red and his son Leif Eriksson were different. When these Vikings sailed into the uncharted waters west of Iceland, they were seeking a different kind of treasure. These Vikings were explorers. They had heard stories about strange lands beyond the horizon. They wanted to find these new lands and see if the stories were true.

At the time of the Vikings, seafaring, or sailing across the ocean, was difficult and dangerous. There were no accurate maps and no modern navigation tools. Most sailors preferred to sail along the coastline. By staying within sight of land, sailors could look for well-known sights, or landmarks. Navigating by landmarks kept sailors from getting lost.

Viking explorers, however, sailed their ships far from the coastline. Their voyages across the Atlantic Ocean to Greenland and North America required these explorers to travel far from land for many days. How did they know where to go? Here are their methods.

PATTERNS OF CLOUDS

Viking explorers knew that clouds tend to form over land. By looking for banks of clouds in the distance, sailors where able to tell when land was nearby.

NEW TOOLS

Viking explorers may have invented a simple navigation tool. This tool is a wooden disk, known as a sun compass. Some scientists think Viking sailors used this tool to find their position or latitude. In other words, it showed sailors how far north or south they were. Only two possible sun compass disks have ever been found. Other scientists do not think the disks were used for this.

VIKING VOYAGE

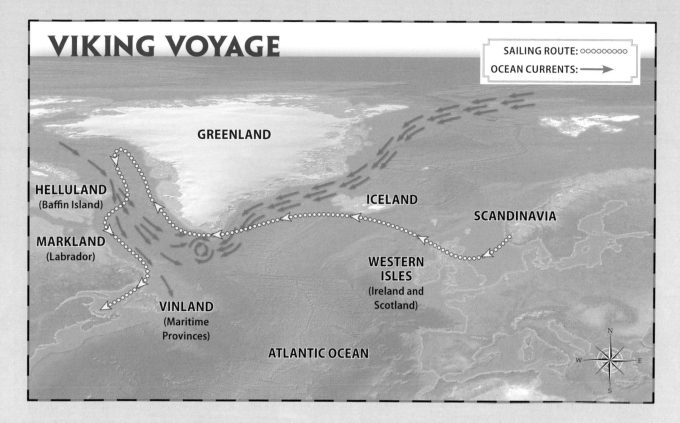

SAILING ROUTE: ooooooooo
OCEAN CURRENTS: ⟶

GREENLAND

HELLULAND
(Baffin Island)

MARKLAND
(Labrador)

ICELAND

SCANDINAVIA

WESTERN
ISLES
(Ireland and
Scotland)

VINLAND
(Maritime
Provinces)

ATLANTIC OCEAN

WINDS AND CURRENTS

Viking explorers knew that the winds and ocean currents of the North Atlantic move in a steady direction. Sailors realized when they followed these winds and currents, they arrived in the same place at the end of each voyage.

SUN AND STARS

Sailors have always used the sun and stars to find the direction they want to follow. The sun moves across the sky from east in the morning to west at night. And at night, the star Polaris shows sailors where the direction north is.

Viking sun compass

FLIGHT OF BIRDS

Many North Atlantic birds spend a lot of time at sea but breed on land. So when sailors saw these birds, they knew they could follow the birds to find land.

Atlantic Puffin

Sailing into the unknown waters of the North Atlantic was terrifying and dangerous. But Viking explorers were willing to take the risk. They hoped to find new lands where they could build settlements. They hoped their discoveries would make them both rich and famous. And they simply wanted to find out what lay beyond the horizon.

Viking Quest

Answer these questions to begin your own voyage of discovery.

1 Why did people fear the Vikings?

2 Describe life in Viking villages and farms.

3 What was special about Viking ships?

4 Name three navigation methods Viking explorers used during their voyages.

5 How did Viking explorers make history?